# CONTENTS

# INTRODUCTION

Obviously in many ways, a lot of things have changed over the course of 100 years. But in some other ways, not much has changed at all. One example of the latter is that of the female celebrity. People love them now just like they did in the 1910s. And we're here to prove it.

Hollywood has become a prominent symbol of the entertainment business, referencing the United States film industry. With blockbuster movies and revolutionary movies released on a regular basis, there's no risk of running out of stuff to watch. The actors and actresses in the films are the main reason we love watching movies so much. Their moving performances in different roles can leave us in tears, with the hair on the backs of our necks standing on end, rendering us completely speechless and making our bodies become riddled with goosebumps. While awards and nominations can certainly advance an actress or actor's career, it does not necessarily define what makes them influential.

The awards recognize an actor or an actress for their performance in a specific role. The criteria by which this is judged may vary. With fans however, the success of a movie, or the amount of awards received are not necessarily what determines an actor's success. Instead, actors are judged by how influential they are over a period of time. This can be determined by the actor's performance or the character in the movie itself. It can also be determined by the number of roles an actor has over a period of time.

Cult movies are not usually the most recognized, as they can be unpopular with mainstream audiences, but they can influence the public because they can still be revolutionary and have a passionate fan base. So when an actor or actress stars in a cult classic, they can be considered influential. The lives of celebrities away from the screen also determines their influence with the public. Their charitable acts and social presence and standing plays a role in how influential they are. With all these different criteria, a celebrity's influence can rise and fall repeatedly. Some of them, however, maintain consistent favor to fans for up to a decade. With that being said, let us take a look at some of the most influential female celebrities of the two eras.

# THE MOST INFLUENTIAL FEMALE CELEBRITIES OF THE 1910S

The 1910s were one of the earliest years of Hollywood's existence. With movies still being a new industry, acting was not what it is today. Regardless, the celebrities of this era had an influence on the masses. They may not be the most famous names in the contemporary world, but they were very influential back in the 1910s. Some of the most influential female celebrities of the era include:

## Marie Dressler

Marie Dressler was a Canadian stage and screen actress and a comedian. Popularly referred to as the queen of silent movies, she began acting before she was 15 years old. At the young age of just 14 years old, Dressler left home and joined a traveling theater troupe that went by the name of the Nevada Stock Company, claiming she was 18 in order to be accepted. Many of her performances took place in the American Midwest, and as she developed her skills, she went on to join different troupes.

In 1892, she started a career on Broadway with one of her most notable roles as the main character in the first ever full-length screen comedy, Tillie's Punctured Romance. The film was so popular that it inspired two sequels, Tillie's Tomato Surprise in 1916 and Tillie Wakes Up the year after that, both of which maintained Dressler as the star. Dressler had actually originally hoped to become an operatic diva or a dramatic actress in tragedy films, but was convinced to accept the reality of where her talent lied, which was with comedic roles. No matter her wages, Dressler stayed consistent in sending money back home to her mother. Eventually, when she reached earnings at $50 per week, she made enough money to be able to fully support her parents and buy them a house on Long Island.

Dressler's love life was nothing short of rocky and troubled. As a teenager, she was a victim of a brief and unhappy marriage. Her second "marriage" with her manager, Jim Dalton, was one of deceit. She had believed that his divorce and their marriage was legitimate. However, when Dalton took the money Dressler gave him for his divorce, he used it to stage a fake marriage with her. When she found out, she threw him out, but still took care of him after he suffered a stroke. During Dressler's last years of her life, she surrounded herself with women, particularly women in the entertainment industry, whose friendships and company gave her lasting happiness. It was also noted that her relationship with a woman named Claire Dubrey was "just shy of openly lesbian," according to Betty Lee from the University Press of Kentucky.

In the 1920s, Dressler's career began declining. She had set out to become her own producer through the Marie Dressler Motion Picture Corporation, but the business failed before it could really even get off the ground. Dressler was left bankrupt and spent the war years selling bonds or working as an entertainer for small events. She could not find any substantial roles because her image was now considered far too old fashioned and undesirable compared to the rising young and glamorous stars of the Jazz

Age. But she blew up again in 1927 with her role in the comedy The Patsy and won the Academy Award for Best Actress for her performance in the 1930 comedy film, Min and Bill. However, her success was cut short when she was diagnosed with terminal cancer.

Dressler's acting roles brought her recognition. She appeared in more than 40 films, and she was one of the stand-out actresses of the industry. She went on to act in the sound era and remains one of the most identifiable names during that period. She was not considered to be the most beautiful actress, since she was bigger in size than the typical Hollywood star, but her talent was undeniable; her hefty frame and booming voice was what set her apart from other celebrities in the industry and made her an actress of unique quality.

*"Her stardom is one of the great anomalies in Hollywood history, a kind of adoration that isn't supposed to happen to an older, homely woman."*

-Matthew Kennedy, author

Dressler died of cancer in 1934. Unlike most other actors of her era, she died during a high point of her career. What Dressler has accomplished has been virtually unheard of in the film and acting business. She rose from the ashes of poverty into fame and success and then experienced a seemingly devastating lull, only to then have her career revived to be better than ever. Dressler proved to the world that even though she possessed an unconventional body type and style, she could still hold her own against the traditionally beautiful actors and actresses of her time. Upon her death, she left $35,000 to her maid Mamie Steele Cox and $15,000 to her butler, who was also Mamie's husband. Dressler wanted the funds to be used to give a place for Black travelers to rest in comfort.

## Mabel Normand

Mabel Normand's roles were mainly in the comedy genre. She starred in at least 167 film shorts and 23 full-length features and was one of the earliest silent actors to serve as her own director. Normand is also credited for her extraordinary contributions to cinema and slapstick comedy. One of her trademark acting techniques includes confiding in the audience and breaking the fourth wall. She played the role of damsel in distress, but also could flip the script and act as the female hero saving a man in trouble, in a time when it was new to see women doing such a thing.

She entered the film industry at a young age as well, at only 16 years old. But before that, she worked as a model, posing for postcard illustrations and clothing catalogs. Her performance in the 1911 short film Her Awakening, was well received and what put her into the spotlight. Normand was thought of as a classic Hollywood beauty, but her knack for comedy prevailed and that is what she became known for. This era was a period in the film industry when women were not thought to be funny, yet she still climbed her way up in the industry and starred in numerous comedy movies. Normand proved to the world that women can be more than just a pretty face. She is also considered to be the first film star to hurl a pie on screen. At the peak of her career in the late 1910s and early 1920s, she had her own movie studio and production company.

Starring alongside comedy greats like Charlie Chaplin in 12 successful films, she is one of the most recognizable faces of the 1910s. Normand actually played a huge part in turning Chaplin into the success that he turned out to be. At first, Chaplin had a hard time adjusting to film acting and it showed in his work, but Normand came to his rescue. She acted as his mentor and besides acting alongside him, she co-wrote and directed films with him.

She also stood up for him when directors expressed their doubts about his performance skills and persuaded them to give him a chance to grow into his roles.

*"She was a kiss that explodes in a laugh; cherry bon-bons in a clown's cap; sharing a cream puff from your best girl; a slap from a perfumed hand."*

-Julian Johnson, lyrical critic at Photoplay

Normand was involved in multiple scandals, effectively drawing attention to herself. The first one involved her co-star, Roscoe Arbuckle, who was accused of manslaughter and rape. Arbuckle was found not guilty, but the scandal still ruined his career. Although Normand was not actually a part of the scandal, she was still associated with him through their work together and the negative media attention Arbuckle received, impacted her career as well.

The second scandal involved the death of one of her directors, William Desmond Taylor. Normand had sought out Taylor for help for her drug addiction. After he resolved to take action against Normand's cocaine suppliers, Taylor was murdered. Newspapers did not miss a chance to spread gossip and embellish stories, claiming that Normand was a "dope fiend" and that Desmond was killed by one of her dealers. Normand was the last person to see him alive, therefore she was subjected to an intense round of questioning by the authorities. She was not considered a suspect in his death, but her career and reputation had already been tainted by these unpleasant matters.

Lastly, in 1924, Normand's chauffeur shot and severely injured a millionaire in the oil industry, Courtland S. Dines, using her pistol. As a result, several theaters pulled Normand's films from distribution and her films were even banned in Ohio. Despite these setbacks, Normand continued to make films with Hal Roach

Studios in 1926. There, she made the films Raggedy Rose, The Nickel-Hopper, and One Hour Married, which was her last film. Her health had begun declining due to tuberculosis, and at the age of 37, she passed away. Normand has a star on the Hollywood Walk of Fame and is consistently referenced in multiple TV shows, movies and songs of today. For example, she was mentioned in an episode of Downton Abbey, and singer Stevie Nicks wrote a song about the actress with the title Mabel Normand. It can be found on Nicks' 2014 album, 24 Karat Gold: Songs from the Vault.

## Mary Pickford

Pickford was a Canadian-American actress and film producer. Her career lasted a whopping 50 years. In the early days of her acting career, she traveled around the U.S alongside her mother and two younger siblings, Lottie and Jack, who were also actors, but only Pickford had the will and desire to become a star. When she started in theater, she was only seven years old. In between gigs, she began looking for work in moving pictures at the Biograph Company in 1909, although she had no intention of staying permanently, as her heart belonged on the stage. Before long, she came to enjoy film acting, and stuck with it, leaving the stage behind. When feature films were introduced in 1913, Pickford met them with great success.

Her film, Tess of the Storm Country (1914), rocked the nation and turned her into an international sensation with die-hard fans everywhere. Probably the most outstanding performer of the 1910s with numerous movies to her name, she set the record for the highest-paid actress, as she was able to negotiate her way into earning a weekly wage of $10,000, 50 percent of her film profits and getting her own production company. She was in control, or at least had a say, in every aspect of the movies she was involved in. This was a time when actresses were not at all well paid or able to obtain positions of power, but Pickford changed that. She starred in almost 50 films throughout the decade, was one of the most identifiable faces on TV, and had a hand in writing and editing scripts. Some of the best features of her career include: Poor Little Rich Girl (1917), Stella Maris (1918), and The Hoodlum (1919). She would also famously be known as America's sweetheart and for her symbolic golden curls.

Pickford used her prominence to do good for a variety of causes. Even though she was America's sweetheart, the very image of innocence and delicateness, she was a well-known philanthropist and strong business woman in an industry dominated by men. During the first World War, she gave speeches at the White House and at Wall Street to promote the sale of Liberty bonds. She was a powerful figure and able to sway the masses toward her favor. The U.S Army named two cannons after her and declared her as an honorary colonel.

In 1916, she helped co-found the Hollywood Studio Club, which was a dormitory for young women in the motion picture industry. After the war, Pickford created the Motion Picture Relief Fund, an organization to help financially struggling actors. Eventually, the fund led to the building of the Motion Picture Country House and Hospital in Woodland Hills, California. In 1919, when she was only 27 years old, Pickford co-founded United Artists, the first independent film distribution company, alongside Charlie Chaplin, D.W Griffith, and her soon-to-be husband, Douglas Fairbanks. Fairbanks and Pickford's marriage resonated positively with fans, as they were considered to be the very image of a perfect fairytale romance. The couple was dubbed the king and queen of Hollywood. In the end, their marriage dissolved due to too much publicity and Pickford's busy schedule. By 1929, the film industry had moved on from silent films, and Pickford was not too ecstatic about the shift.

*"She thought that sound was a terrible idea, that movies*

> *were an art in the silent form. And she said it was like putting lipstick on the Venus de Milo."*

-Doe Mayer, professor at USC's School of Cinematic Arts

Pickford attempted two sound films before the decade ended, Coquette (1929) and Taming of the Shrew (1929). While Coquette did win her an Academy Award for Best Actress, her sound films simply were not as good as her silent pictures. Finally, Pickford retired in 1933 and turned to alcohol like her father did. Her siblings had also died of alcohol-related causes in the 1930s. However, she did not have idle hands and managed to stay busy during retirement. In 1955, she published a memoir called Sunshine and Shadows. This was not her only work of published writing. She had previously published a 1934 essay about spirituality and personal growth called Why Not Try God and an essay in 1935 detailing her beliefs on an afterlife and death, titled My Rendezvous of Life. Not to mention, she also wrote a novel, The Demi-Widow, in 1935. In 1979, she died at the ripe age of 87.

Mary Pickford left quite a legacy behind. Numerous schools, hospitals, and other organizations have named themselves after her in her honor and high profile film festivals still show her movies, or other productions based off of her work, as recently as 2017. Her philanthropic work has also been highly praised, especially given her impoverished upbringing. As a person of compassion and grace, Pickford was highly attuned to human suffering. Her background of poverty did not cause her to hoard her money for herself, instead she decided to help others. That is what makes Pickford so memorable as an actress.

## Pola Negri

Pola Negri, a Polish woman by birth, excelled as a stage actress in Poland before moving to America. She was the first European actress to be signed on to Hollywood after Paramount Pictures offered her a film contract. Her roles in the 1910s were not as abundant as other actresses, but she would still be fondly remembered. Her ascension to fame was largely propelled by rumors about her supposed love affairs with Charlie Chaplin, Rod La Rocque, Rudolph Valentino and even Adolf Hitler at one point.

Growing up, Negri lived a life full of hardships. She comes from impoverished Polish nobility; her mother's family had lost their fortune. With Negri's father arrested by Russian authorities and banished to Siberia, Negri's mother was barely scraping by. Negri's introduction to theater began with her admittance into the Warsaw Imperial Academy of Dramatic Arts. By the end of the first World War, she had already risen to moderate fame and established herself as a popular stage actress. Her popularity in Poland gave her an opportunity to move to Germany, where she starred in many successful hits like The Eyes of the Mummy Ma (Die Augen der Mumie Ma, 1918), Carmen (1918) and Madame DuBarry (1919). The latter two films were reissued in the U.S and were so idolized that they threatened Hollywood's position as the film and entertainment empire. This was why Hollywood was so eager to recruit her.

When she moved to America, Negri became a crowd favorite and was known as the queen of tragedy. Aside from her legendary movies, she started fashion trends in Hollywood, many of which are still in use today. For example, red painted toenails, turbans and fur boots. Her first two films with Paramount were Bella Donna (1923) and The Cheat (1923). Negri's status as a foreigner led Paramount to paint her as a mysterious femme fatale, Hollywood's first. She also became a famous sex symbol. Negri was worried that Paramount was ruining her image, so they cast her in roles that were meant to be more relatable to the general public. Of course, the company's efforts came too little, too late as viewers had already begun to grow tired of Negri's depiction on screen. While some of her movies like The Crown of Lies (1926) and Hotel Imperial (1927) garnered positive reactions, her 1926 film, Good and Naughty, received unfavorable reviews. And in 1927, Barbed Wire was a flop, apparently due to her behavior at her fiancé's, Rudolph Valentino's, funeral.

Negri's behavior at the funeral was interpreted as overly hysterical and excessive to the vastly American crowd, despite the fact that she was simply mourning over her dead husband-to-be. Back in 1926 in Motion Picture Magazine, director Herbert Brenon described her as "sensitive to impressions" and "very temperamental." Negri defended her behavior by saying that she comes from a whole different culture where things are perceived differently.

> *"It is difficult for a foreigner coming to America...I had been told so much what not to do. It was particularly difficult for me, a Slav. My emotion seemed exaggerated to Americans. I cannot help that I haven't the Anglo-Saxon restraint and tact."*

-Pola Negri

In 1928, Negri made her last film with Paramount, The Woman from Moscow, and decided to enter into retirement. However, her retirement from film did not last very long. She found out that her husband was gambling away her fortune and so, she went back to acting and made her last silent film, The Way of Lost Souls (1929). She returned to Hollywood in 1931 to film her first movie with sound and talking. The movie was titled A Woman Commands (1932) and in all honesty, was not well received. After a brief stint in Hollywood, she went to Germany where she appeared in the film Mazurka (1935). It was revered in Germany; it even came to knowledge that it was one of Hitler's favorite films, sparking a rumor that Negri and Hitler were having an affair, effectively sweeping the nation off its feet. Negri actually sued the French magazine that had started the rumor, and won. The Polish actress retired for good in 1945, but came out of retirement briefly in 1948 to take part in Walt Disney's film, The Moon-Spinners (1964). She died in 1987 at the age of 90. The cause of her death was pneumonia and an untreated brain tumor.

Negri was a very accomplished woman. She received an honorary award from the German film industry and a Hemis-Film award in San Antonio. She also overcame many barriers. Navigating a completely new culture in America and adjusting to the language was not easy, yet she flourished. Besides that, she had to deal with widespread gossip over her personal life and the false image of herself that the media perpetuated. As Hollywood's first femme fatale, she gave rise to countless films and TV shows with female characters inspired by and modeled after her, creating an entirely new category of movie genres.

## Lillian Gish

Lillian Gish is a native of Springfield, Ohio. She turned to acting along with her mother and her sister, Dorothy, to support their family. Her father was an absent parent who left her with few choices. Once she made her on screen debut, though, she had found her calling. She would star in over 100 movies throughout her time in the entertainment business, and would float her way to the top. Her acting career lasted a span of 75 years. Her best but also most controversial film, due to its depictions of racism, is considered to be The Birth of a Nation (1915). Other popular films include Intolerance (1916), Broken Blossoms (1919), Way Down East (1920), and Orphans of the Storm (1921).

Eventually, Gish and her family moved to New York where she became close friends with Mary Pickford. Pickford was the one who helped kickstart Gish's career. In 1912, she introduced Gish and her sister to director D.W Griffith and got them contracts with Biograph Studios. Gish would remain friends with Pickford for the rest of her life. Gish became known as the First Lady of American cinema. She directed one movie in all her years of acting. It starred her sister Dorothy in Remodeling Her Husband (1920). She never directed again and in that same year in an interview with Photoplay, she made the implication that directing was a man's job. "I am not strong enough to direct. I doubt if any woman is."

It is hard to tell whether she genuinely believed that women were incapable or if her remark was simply made to further cultivate her image. While Gish had a reputation for being innocent and fragile, she showed remarkable resourcefulness and tact. But it is also possible that she could've had a hand in establishing what became the normal division of labor with women acting and men in the director's chair. In her lesser known 1930 essay, In Defense of the Silent Film, she lists the names of directors she considered to be important, and all of them are men.

Gish was a woman who was not hungry for money. In fact, she cared about the quality of her films more than anything else. In 1925, MGM offered her a million dollars to sign on with them, but she actually asked for a lower wage in order to have more funds to boost the quality of the films.

> *"In the theater, I played with the best actors and tried never to get caught acting. I was never interested in money... I just wanted films I'd be proud of because I felt they were permanent and I didn't want to apologize for any of them."*

-Lillian Gish

At MGM, she starred in La Boheme (1926), The Scarlet Letter (1926), and The Wind (1928) where she had the creative freedom to make substantial contributions in the films' production. After that, she kept a low profile in movie acting, coming out with the occasional film. From the 1950s to late 1980s, Gish mainly focused on television and radio. Her most renowned work in TV was her leading role in The Trip to Bountiful (1953). Her last film role was in The Whales of August (1987) at age 93.

Gish received many awards for her incredible work. At different times throughout her life, she won the Special Academy Award, the Women in Film Crystal Award, and the American Film Institute Lifetime Achievement Award. She was the second woman ever to receive this award. She also received the National Board of Review Award for Best Actress, the George Eastman Award for distinguished contributions to the art of film, the Academy Honorary Award, and an AFI Life Achievement Award. Gish died of heart failure in 1993 at age 99. The AllMovie Guide wrote of her legacy:

*"A pioneer of fundamental film performing techniques, she was the first star to recognize the many crucial differences between acting for the stage and acting for the screen...Gish delivered finely etched, nuanced turns carrying a stunning emotional impact. While by no means the biggest or most popular actress of the silent era, she was the most gifted, her seeming waiflike frailty masking unparalleled reserves of physical and spiritual strength."*

# THE MOST INFLUENTIAL FEMALE CELEBRITIES OF THE 2010S

Fast forward a hundred years later, and Hollywood is a much different industry. Women now get the credit they deserve for their roles, and they are phenomenal. They are as influential as their male counterparts, and they do just as much work if not more. With music and other forms of entertainment now recognizing female members, the list is diverse. Here are some of the top female celebrities of the 2010s.

## Beyoncé

Famously known by the nickname of "Queen B," Beyoncé is widely regarded as the undisputed queen of the music industry. Her musical performances are known for sold out arenas, and her dancing ability is through the roof. She is a strong advocate for female participation in all different fields. She has been a household name for close to 20 years now, and she is still going. In particular, her albums Beyoncé and Lemonade were two of the most influential and highly discussed releases of the past ten years. She has also starred in numerous movies across the decade such as The Pink Panther, Dreamgirls, Obsessed  and The Lion King in 2019.

Beyoncé was born and raised in Houston, Texas and is married to rapper Jay-Z. The couple often collaborate together on their music. They have three kids together, Blue Ivy Carter and twins, Sir Carter and Rumi. Beyoncé rose to fame in the world of music as the lead singer of Destiny's Child, one of the best selling girl groups of all time. Beyoncé went on to form her own solo career and released her first album Dangerously in Love in 2003. Her two hit singles from the album, "Baby Boy" and "Crazy in Love," which we all know and love, were on the U.S Billboard Hot 100 and topped the charts, both making it to claim the number one spot. After that, she released her second album in 2006 called B'Day, which produced her next hit singles, "Irreplaceable" and "Beautiful Liar." Her third album I Am... Sasha Fierce, released in 2008, was arguably her most successful, bearing the still-popular songs "If I Were a Boy, "Single Ladies (Put a Ring on It)" and "Halo."

Her other later albums include 4 (2011), Beyoncé (2013), Lemonade (2016) and Everything is Love (2018). Lemonade was the world's best selling album of the year. It was surrounded with themes of infidelity and spoke of her husband's alleged affair with a mystery mistress. Beyoncé is undeniably one of the most successful musical artists in the world. In 2014, Billboard named her as the highest earning Black musician of all time. Beyoncé's music style generally consists of pop, R&B, and hip hop although there are times when she incorporates soul and funk into her songs. Her music typically includes themes of female empowerment. Her style changed the nature of music and is often mimicked in other songs of today. Additionally, she has coined popular phrases such as "put a ring on it" and "I woke up like this." At one point, the latter phrase could be found inscribed on t-shirts in almost every clothing store. Beyoncé has also become a major sex symbol. Her revealing outfits and luscious curves caused the media to literally invent a new word to describe her, which was "bootylicious." It was added to the Oxford English Dictionary in 2006. Beyoncé explored other endeavors besides movies and music. She has multiple endorsements from big brands like Pepsi and is involved in the fashion industry as well. In 2014, she launched an activewear line with Topshop and now owns the brand. She is also a partner with Adidas and develops clothes for them.

Beyoncé has received awards upon awards for her music, almost too many to count. Back in 2002, she received Songwriter of the Year from American Society of Composers, Authors and Publishers, becoming the first African American woman to win the award. Five years later, she won the International Artist of Excellence Award by the American Music Awards. She also has received a Career Achievement Award, a Fashion Icon Award, Mother of the Year award  and has been named artist of the decade. Her most recent achievement was in 2020 when she was presented with the BET Humanitarian Award. Overall, the singer has a grand total of 28 Grammy Awards and 24 MTV Video Music Awards, making her the most awarded artist in music history. In addition, Beyoncé has been declared by BBC Radio to be one of the most influential women in the past 70 years.

Aside from creating catchy hit singles and making music history, Beyoncé is known for her philanthropic gestures. She has made an immense difference in countless lives and donated millions of dollars to a variety of charities including but not limited to: hurricane relief organizations and other natural disasters, rehabilitation organizations, the Black Lives Matter movement and provided resources and assistance to the American people during the COVID-19 pandemic. Beyoncé provided relief for individuals who lost their homes due to natural disasters, particularly during Hurricane Katrina, Hurricane Ike, Hurricane Harvey, Hurricane Matthew, and the devastating earthquakes in Haiti. She later worked with Phoenix House, a nonprofit drug and alcohol rehab organization, to which she donated her entire salary of $4 million from her movie Cadillac Records. Beyoncé and her mother even established the Beyoncé Cosmetology Center for the patients of Phoenix House to help them get back on their feet and gain new skills for potential careers after recovery. Beyoncé and her husband also bailed many Black Lives Matter protesters out of jail and have previously donated substantial amounts of money to the cause.

In 2020, when the coronavirus pandemic stunned the nation into fear and anxiety, Beyoncé donated $6 million to the National Alliance in Mental Health and other mental health organizations so essential workers could access the resources they needed during those difficult and unprecedented times. She also partnered up with many local organizations to provide food, water, face masks and more to communities of color, knowing that the virus outbreak would disproportionately harm them. Beyoncé also has made an incredible impact on the wellbeing of Black owned small businesses. In July of 2020, she established the Black Owned Small Business Impact Fund, which offers $10,000 grants to struggling businesses. She donated an additional $1 million to the fund two months later. In December of 2020, the singer donated $500,000 to help with the housing crisis taking over the U.S.

Beyoncé is a celebrity who has gone above and beyond to help people in need. She was even named Most Charitable Celebrity of the year in 2016. It is clear that Beyoncé is not the type of person who does good deeds just for recognition or awards. Even though she is extremely wealthy and can spend her money on more fancy cars than she needs or purchase multiple vacation homes, she chooses not to, refusing to forget about her fans who helped get her to where she is today. She knows she has a certain privilege and uses it to help out the less fortunate. She truly cares about the people on this earth and wants nothing more than to ease human suffering. Beyoncé not only serves as an entertainer, that is, she doesn't just make music to fulfill her passion or acquire loads of money, she uses her earnings from her music to give aid to those in need.

## Margot Robbie

Margot Robbie is an Australian actress. She wasn't a big star until she landed a role in Wolf of Wall Street (2013) with Leonardo DiCaprio. While other actresses may have faded into obscurity, she has risen even higher since then. With roles alongside renowned actors like Will Smith, she is a massive star. Her role as comic book character Harley Quinn in Suicide Squad (2016) made men and women alike go crazy at the time. Robbie was actually the first person to portray the DC Comics villain, so the pressure was on for her to play the character spectacularly and accurately. She worked hard while preparing for the role of Harley Quinn, practicing all kinds of gymnastics, boxing, and holding her breath underwater for five minutes at a time. She even performed most of her own stunts in the film, leaving her stunt double with little to do. Her efforts did not go unnoticed. Suicide Squad was a giant success with global revenues of over $700 million. She has since reprised the role in Birds of Prey and James Gunn's The Suicide Squad (2021). Other iconic movies of hers include About Time (2013), Once Upon a Time in Hollywood (2019), Z for Zachariah (2015) and I, Tonya (2017). She is also a major Hollywood producer, putting her own money behind projects like Birds of Prey, Promising Young Woman (2020), and an upcoming Barbie film.

Robbie started out her acting career on the famous Aussie soap opera Neighbors. Before that, she was involved in low-budget independent films. Robbie was a born actress. Ever since childhood, she was constantly putting on shows for her family. She recalls making her family pay to watch her shows.

*"I was really dramatic... I was obsessed with movies with anything on TV and whatever I saw, I would re-enact it for my mum who had enough on her plate running a house, looking after four kids and I'd be pulling at her leg..."*

-Margot Robbie

When she moved to America to pursue acting, she was praised for her American accent, particularly her New York accent, which she often used in her films. She is an actress of diversity, excelling in the categories of drama, comedy and action. Time magazine named her one of the 100 most influential people in the world in 2017 and The Hollywood Reporter declared her as one of the 100 most powerful people in the entertainment industry and one of the 100 most influential women in entertainment in 2021. Robbie also is known for promoting feminism, women's rights and the work of women. In 2016, Robbie took on the role of Jane Porter in an adaptation of Tarzan called The Legend of Tarzan. Surrounded by an all-male cast and keeping in mind the previous portrayals of the original Jane, Robbie was bent on making sure that the Jane she would be playing was not merely a damsel in distress, but a woman who actively looked for a way out in a pinch instead of waiting for a man to save her. Robbie also refused to lose weight for the role, thinking that it was unnecessary just because she is a woman. In 2018, she backed the charity, Time Up, in their mission to protect women from harassment and discrimination.

Robbie is married to British filmmaker Tom Ackerley. Together they are founders of the production company LuckyChap Entertainment where Robbie focuses on producing female-oriented films. She has also lent a hand to several other communities that are in need of recognition or financial support. In 2014, and in more recent years, she was involved in a fundraising campaign with the Motion Picture and Television Fund, which helps people in the film and TV industries that lack resources. Furthermore, Robbie has offered support to families and refugees who are victims of war and other hardships. In 2016, she joined the UN Refugee Agency to increase awareness and gather more public support for families running from conflicts in their home countries. Later that same year, she donated $50,000 to UNICEF to help refugee children. In April of 2021, Robbie received the RAD Impact Award. She decided to share the prize with a charity called Youngcare, and as a result, a donation was made for the purpose of aiding young people with higher care needs.

For her acting, Robbie has won two awards: Best International Lead Actress for her film I, Tonya and Best Supporting Actress for Bombshell (2019). She has been nominated for many more awards including Academy Awards, four Golden Globes, and five Screen Actors Guild Awards. Robbie may seemingly have risen to fame quickly and in the easiest way possible, but her status as a powerful and influential actress did not happen in the blink of an eye. Being an amazing actress takes time, hard work and constant practicing of skills, something that she feels she needs to remind her awestruck fans.

*"Everyone's like an 'overnight sensation.' It's not overnight. It's years of hard work."*

-Margot Robbie

## Lupita Nyong'o

Lupita Nyong'o is a Kenyan-Mexican actress who rose to stardom in 2013 for her award-winning performance in 12 Years A Slave. She has since followed that with incredible performances in Black Panther (2018) and Us (2019). She is also a major activist, constantly fighting for women's rights, animal rights, and historic preservation. Nyong'o was born in Mexico City and moved to the U.S for college, earning a bachelor's degree in film and theater studies from Hampshire College. She began her career as a production assistant in Hollywood, working on films like The Constant Gardener (2005), The Namesake (2006) and Where God Left His Shoes (2007). She later went on to pursue a master's degree in acting from the Yale School of Drama. Shortly after her graduation, she landed a role in Steve McQueen's 12 Years a Slave, for which she won the Academy Award for Best Supporting Actress, becoming the first African, Kenyan and Mexican actress to win the award. Before her attendance at the Yale School of Drama, Nyong'o had a few smaller but successful projects. In 2008, she made her acting debut with the short film East River and then returned to Kenya to star in Shuga, a television drama series that lasted for three years. She also wrote, produced and directed a documentary called In My Genes (2009), detailing the discrimination toward Kenya's albino population. The documentary was played at several film festivals and even won a first prize award.

After 12 Years a Slave, Nyong'o was involved in the film Non-Stop (2014) and co-starred in Star Wars: The Force Awakens (2015). She then took to theater and landed a starring role in the play Eclipsed (2015), which won her an Obie Award for Outstanding Performance and a Theater World Award. The play was the first to premiere on Broadway with an all-black and all-female cast and crew. Nyong'o is undoubtedly a hardworking actress. In one of her other most prominent roles, Black Panther, she learned to speak an entirely new language and learned judo, jujitsu, and Filipino martial arts, all in preparation for her part. For her role in Jordan Peele's Us, she won an NAACP Image Award for Best Actress. Nyong'o is an actress who is not afraid to embrace her blackness. She narrated a Discovery Channel documentary series about Serengeti wildlife. She was inspired to do so because she noticed a lack of African women narrating nature documentaries. She even used her Kenyan accent on the series. Nyong'o has many upcoming projects that she is working on. She is projected to star in a spy/thriller film called The 355 (2022). Additionally, she plans to star in a TV series based on a novel, Americanah, and a film adaptation of Born In a Crime. Furthermore, the actress will reprise the role of the character Nakia in the sequel Black Panther: Wakanda Forever, which is scheduled to release in July of 2022.

Nyong'o has appeared on the cover of a variety of magazines and is reputed for her beauty as a Black woman. 2014 was an especially big year for her. She was on New York's spring fashion issue and the UK magazine Dazed and Confused. People magazine named her as "The Most Beautiful Woman" and Glamour named her "Woman of the Year." She became the new face of Lancome that year, making her the first Black woman ever to appear on the brand. She also appeared on the cover of Vogue, making her the second African woman to cover the magazine. She then appeared on the cover of Elle magazine's July issue. Nyong'o also has an official day named after her in her honor. It has been deemed "Lupita Nyong'o Day." In 2017, she appeared on the cover of Vogue for the fourth time, which made her the first Black actress to do so.

Aside from having amazing acting skills, Nyong'o can speak four languages fluently: English, Spanish, Luo and Swahili. She is also passionate about preserving historical sites. In 2014, she worked with the National Trust for Historic Preservation to prevent the development of a baseball stadium on a major slave trading site in Richmond, Virginia. In 2015, she went back to Kenya to work with the conservation organization, WildAid, to protect the elephants and raise awareness on women's issues as well as promote the importance of the arts. Later on, she started an anti-poaching campaign to spread knowledge on the endangerment of elephants and rhinos, animals that are constantly hunted for their ivory tusks and horns. Nyong'o is also involved with Mother Health International, an organization with the mission to provide relief to women and children via birthing centers.

Nyong'o is not just an actress, but a writer as well. In the wake of the Harvey Weinstein scandal, she wrote a story for The New York Times revealing that she had been sexually harassed by Weinstein twice, forcing her to refuse any roles in films that he was involved in. A few years later, she wrote a book titled Sulwe (2019), which follows the story of a young Kenyan girl with dark skin. The book won the award for Outstanding Literary Work – Children. Nyong'o is a wonderful role model for young girls of color. It is important to see more diverse faces in Hollywood to show that Black women can accomplish anything and more. She is part of the mission to make Black faces in the media the norm. Her journey is inspiring, and although she faced discrimination along the way, she did not let that stop her.

*"It's really not exceptional to be black, or to be African, and I think that's a powerful statement in and of itself. We can be seen and perceived as part and parcel of the global experience, because that is the truth."*

-Lupita Nyong'o, The New York Times

## Emma Watson

Everyone knows and loves Hermione Granger from Harry Potter, and the actress who plays her is just as beloved. Emma Watson landed this role after only acting in school plays previously. Casting agents and producers were blown away by her talent. Over the years, fans could see how Watson grew and matured in her role as Hermione. She received praise left and right for her performances in each installment of the Harry Potter film series, receiving an abundance of awards. Some of her awards include the Young Artist Award for Leading Young Actress for her performance in Philosopher's Stone, several Otto Awards, the National Movie Award for Best Female Performance and British Artist of the Year.

Although she reached fame and success with her part as Hermione, Watson was still determined to continue her studies. She split her time between filming and school, finally graduating with a bachelor's degree in English literature from Brown University. The English actress has since said goodbye to Hermione and has acquired other notable roles, such as parts in Little Women (2019), The Perks of Being a Wallflower (2012) and Beauty and the Beast (2017). However, she will forever be Hermione to most. Her first professional role outside of Harry Potter was in My Week with Marilyn (2011). But it wasn't until Perks of Being a Wallflower that she received extensive praise again for her role as a flirtatious high schooler. As Belle in Beauty and the Beast, Watson was able to have a say in how she wanted her character to be portrayed. She emphasized Belle's independence and individuality in the movie. Watson earned a salary of over $15 million from the film. After starring in Little Women, she revealed that she wanted to be more lowkey in her work and focus on making more of a difference in people's lives rather than on the entertainment side.

Watson has also dabbled in the fashion industry and participated in modeling. Her modeling career began with a photo shoot for Teen Vogue in 2005, making her the youngest person to grace the cover of the magazine. In February of 2011, she was presented with the Style Icon Award from British Elle. In September 2009, Watson started working with People Tree, a sustainable fashion brand, creating several collections and lines of clothing. Watson had already shown a preference for sustainability early on and is known for her environmentally friendly outfits. For example, at the 2016 Met Gala, she wore a Calvin Klein dress made out of recycled plastic bottles. She has also collaborated with companies to promote ethical clothing and raise awareness of how harmful the clothing industry can be to the environment.

*"Fashion is a great way to empower people and give*

*them skills; rather than give cash to charity you can help people by buying the clothes they make and supporting things they take pride in. I think young people like me are becoming increasingly aware of the humanitarian issues surrounding fast fashion and want to make good choices but there aren't many options out there."*

-Emma Watson

Watson has also gained recognition for her work in women's rights. She has been an outspoken feminist since the beginning. She believes in the importance of girls' education, traveling to countries like Bangladesh and Zambia to promote it. She has also made a visit to Uruguay to speak out about the need for female participation in politics. Watson has been a U.N. Women Goodwill Ambassador since 2014. Being subjected to the public and in front of cameras at such a young age, Watson has experienced criticism regarding her behavior more than most, causing her to quickly learn the difference in treatment between men and women, especially in Hollywood. She revealed that she had already been noticing gender differences since the age of eight, when she was called "bossy" while boys were not. At 14 years old, she was already consistently sexualized in the media. She recalled that on her 18th birthday, paparazzi photographers were attempting to take photos of her underneath her skirt. She also called for men to stand up for gender equality. Watson has endured a lot of backlash for her stance on women's rights and status as a feminist, but that has only empowered her to work harder to spread the message, especially after all she has been through regarding oversexualization. Time listed her as one of the 100 most influential people in the world.

In March of 2017, Watson was accused of hypocrisy for taking part in a Vanity Fair photo shoot where her breasts were partly visible. She argued that feminism is about supporting women in their choices, not tearing them down and that body parts have nothing to do with it. Watson also recognizes the fact that she has white privilege and actually strove to understand the nuances behind it and how whiteness is used to uphold an unfair society. She has donated 1 million euros to the Time's Up foundation based in the U.K, which in turn, helped out communities of women across the country. In July 2019, Watson set up a legal helpline that people who have suffered sexual harassment in the workplace can call for advice, legal or not. Her work did not stop there. The actress has reiterated her support for transgender and nonbinary people alike, after J.K Rowling, the author of the Harry Potter series, expressed harmful comments on gender identity. Watson has been behind projects that highlight women and the LGBTQ community's contributions to history. In addition, Watson has voiced her unending support for Black Lives Matter and tries to educate others about the effects of racism. Her view on women's rights and her efforts in activism has been labeled as the "Emma Watson effect" because many people assert that she was their inspiration to embrace feminism.

Through Harry Potter, Emma Watson is part of a huge series that became a significant part of pop culture, but she did not have her legacy end there with Hermione. The kind-hearted actress is described as shy, friendly and intelligent with a down to earth personality. She is very much against being known just for her wealth and fame, so she strives to create positive change in the world.

## Zendaya Coleman

Zendaya Coleman is an American actress and singer. She started off as a child model with big brands like Old Navy and Macy's and had a few other small dance/performer roles. After gaining recognition in her role as Rocky Blue on the Disney show Shake It Up, she has since become a fan favorite. Her rise to stardom was seemingly instant, following the release of her hit single "Watch Me" with Bella Thorne, which peaked at number 86 on the Billboard Hot 100. Zendaya released other music as well, such as "Swag It Out," " Something to Dance For" and "Fashion is My Kryptonite." In 2013, after signing on with Hollywood Records, she released her album titled Zendaya, which was truly a work of art. Her single, "Replay," was a smash hit. Zendaya's first film role was in Frenemies (2012), a Disney Channel movie. Until 2018, she was still with Disney, acting in a show called K.C Undercover.

Zendaya has now shed her Disney image and has moved on to more adult projects. She played MJ in Spiderman: Homecoming (2017) alongside actor Tom Holland. Zendaya showed up to her audition with a face free of makeup, which was a decision that proved to contribute to her staple looks in the movie. Even in Hollywood, where famous people are supposed to be caught up in appearances and engaged with the glitz and glamour of celebrity lifestyles,  Zendaya proved to be the opposite of that by showing up bare faced. She illustrated that she is not afraid to be her raw, true self. Zendaya then co-starred in The Greatest Showman (2017) with Zac Efron. In 2019, she began starring in Euphoria, an HBO drama series, which is her most popular work yet. In Euphoria, she strayed as far away from her Disney image as she could get. Her character, Rue, is a 17 year old drug addict. Zendaya won the Primetime Emmy Award for Outstanding Lead Actress in a Drama Series for her portrayal of Rue, becoming the youngest person to receive this award. In 2019, she reprised her role of MJ in Spiderman: Far From Home. Then in 2021, she starred in Malcolm & Marie, which was filmed during the beginning stages of the coronavirus pandemic, creating new challenges. Zendaya made sure that everyone involved in the making of the film was paid and paid fairly. She is currently working on a number of film projects including a science fiction film by the name of Dune, Spiderman: No Way Home, and A White Lie.

Zendaya is revered for her knack toward incorporating diversity and inclusion into her work. She includes women of color, plus size models, and older models. Zendaya's shoe collection, Daya, which dropped in 2015, was gender fluid and included all shoe sizes. In 2020, the young actress and singer won the Visionary Award at the CNMI Green Carpet Fashion Awards. She has also represented high end brands like Tommy Hilfiger, Lancome, Covergirl, Bulgari and Valentino. It is clear how impactful she is because everyone wants her to promote their products!

Additionally, Zendaya has lent her support to charities and causes. She primarily dedicates her efforts to the underprivileged and underserved communities. She has raised awareness and money to go toward hurricane relief efforts and focused on feeding the hungry. On her 18th birthday, she partnered up with an organization to help feed hungry children in places like Haiti and the Philippines. A portion of the proceeds from her film Malcolm & Marie also went to Feeding America. Zendaya has also teamed up with Verizon in an effort to bring more access to technology in schools, which would expand kids' learning opportunities. She encourages children to pursue careers in STEM because for so long, that field has been restricted to white men. In 2018, Zendaya teamed up with Google to fund a computer science curriculum for schools in Oakland. Through social media, she has been vocal about women's rights, racial injustice and body shaming. As a young Black female in Hollywood, Zendaya has definitely had her fair share of criticism and racial encounters. She relayed her experience at the 87th Academy Awards. Italian entertainment reporter Giuliana Rancic had made a passing comment meant as a joke, remarking on the scent of Zendaya's hair, stating that it smelled like "patchouli oil" and "weed." Zendaya defended her hairstyle, stating that it had nothing to do with drugs.

> *"There is already harsh criticism of African American hair in society without the help of ignorant people who choose to judge others based on the curl of their hair. My wearing my hair in locs on an Oscar red carpet was to showcase them in a positive light, to remind people of color that our*

*hair is good enough. To me locs are a symbol of beauty and strength, almost like a lion's mane."*

-Zendaya Coleman

It is not an easy task to address racism in Hollywood and the actress definitely has her work cut out for her. She has been consistently showing support for the Black Lives Matter movement for years and took part in the George Floyd protests. Zendaya also encourages her fans to vote, reminding them via social media all the time. She is also aware of the certain privilege she has, saying that she is "Hollywood's acceptable version of a Black woman" because she is more light skinned due to her mixed background. She pushes for more Black representation and turns down roles that she thinks should go to someone with darker skin. Overall, what makes Zendaya such an influential celebrity is that she is not afraid to speak her mind, she's unapologetic, and takes control of her story. We're excited to see more of what she has to offer because at only 24 years old, she really is just getting started.

# AFTERWORD

When looking at the two different decades from two different centuries, there is one thing they have in common, which is the state of poverty. Most of the actresses mentioned in the 1910s category grew up poor and in the 2010s, celebrities are still trying to use their wealth and status to combat poverty around the world. One would think that over a century later, the problem of poverty would have long been solved. Unfortunately, that is not the case. Furthermore, in comparing the female celebrities from the 1910s and the 2010s, we can see that the 2010s gave rise to many more women of color, whereas the 1910s boast strictly white actresses. Any entertainers or performers of that decade who were people of color were men, and even then they were rare. As a society, we have come a long way in the treatment toward people of color. They thankfully have more opportunities and are no longer restricted to oppressive service roles. Society has greatly benefited from their artistic contributions.

While some things may have improved, we can see that others have stayed almost exactly the same. Even though our technology has advanced to entirely new levels and we enjoy many comforts and luxuries that did not exist in the past, several basic fundamental elements of human behavior have not budged. Many of the patterns that played out during the 1910s are still present in today's world. For instance, there is the treatment toward immigrants and people who come from different cultures. In the 1910s, actress Pola Negri, who immigrated to the U.S from Poland, was criticized for her display of sadness and sorrow at her fiancé's funeral. It was considered to be much too emotional.

This response shows how Americans are not really open to understanding aspects of other cultures besides their own. They believe that their way of life is the only way, the one true way. This type of thinking can be seen in the 2010s, as well as more recent years. Black actresses like Lupita Nyong'o and Zendaya who grew up in the contemporary world, still face judgment for aspects of their culture and identity. They receive negative comments about their hair and skin, and are subjected to outdated stereotypes surrounding Black women about their "aggression" and promiscuity.

Moreover, women in general still are victims of the patriarchal values that governed society in previous decades. Their physical appearances determine whether or not they are fit for certain roles both then and now. It seems that in more modern times, society would be able to look past the outside and embrace what's on the inside. Take Marie Dressler, for instance. Her size made her unfit for the roles she truly wanted, even though she displayed remarkable talent and range. Instead, she was forced to settle for comedy roles. Her comedic performances were marvelous and deserve every bit of praise there is to offer, but it does not erase the fact that big women have historically been reduced to large bumbling fools, observed by audiences as circus freaks and regarded as less than human. And today, bigger women like the "Truth Hurts" singer, Lizzo, are dealing with fat shaming despite having a great voice and personality. She has spread nothing but positivity, yet the world is giving her hate because of her weight. Although society may still have retained some of its toxic habits, they are powerless when it comes to dimming the light of these famous multi-talented female celebrities. Hopefully, in the future, we will experience major improvements in terms of treating women equally and with the respect that they deserve.